This Book Belongs to :

_ _

Dear Parents

Welcome to the Ocean Animals Coloring Book! My name is Nouha, I am an engineer and a visual artist passionate about fun and positive learning environments. I have worked with kids for years and decided to contribute with a collection of books carefully developed to enhance your child's creativity, nurture their curiosity, create memories and teach them with joy.

Children between the age of one to eight have awesome energy we as parents need to channel effectively. The Ocean Animals Coloring Book is a great place to start. It can be a "Let's color together" session, where you engage, talk about the day, or simply enjoy a sweet parent-child moment. Or, a solo coloring session, which is profoundly therapeutic and calming.

As children shift their focus to concentrate on finishing their masterpiece, this peaceful activity can provide an outlet for processing emotions and take the focus off challenging situations.

Through these pages, your child will explore, experiment, and learn. Practicing is important to improve fine motor skills, and messy mistakes are crucial and beautiful!

The Ocean Animals Coloring Book contains animals your child may come across at public aquariums, in books, or in documentaries. A page to test colors, and explore choices to improve decision-making skills is attached. All designs are hand-drawn carefully to include different levels of difficulty and purposely made bold for a better coloring experience. Fun facts are included with every animal to nurture vocabulary and start conversations!

Your child will also explore multiple concepts and ideas through hand-drawn activity pages such as mazes and dot-to-dot, providing more than just fun! A completion certificate is attached at the end of the book to color, cut, and keep!

Honest reviews from wonderful customers like you help other parents feel confident about choosing the Ocean Animals Coloring Book. Sharing your experience will be greatly appreciated!

I hope you enjoy the Ocean Animals Coloring Book! Happy Coloring!

-Nouha.H

Color testing

Test your Colors here

Pufferfish can inflate into a ball shape to look bigger and evade predators. Some pufferfish species also have spines on their skin!

Seahorse is a small, upright-swimming fish with a horse-like head! Seahorses have a big appetite, they do not have a stomach, so they must eat often.

Seahorse is a small, upright-swimming fish with a
tails like heart. Seahorses have a big appetite,
they do not have a stomach so they must eat
often.

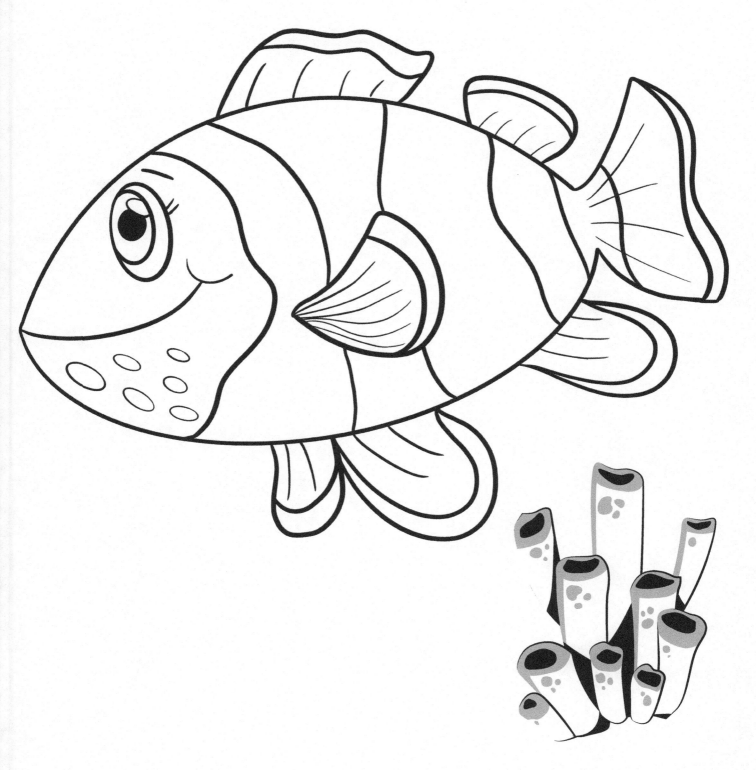

Clownfish is a small tropical fish of the Indian and Pacific Oceans, with orange and white stripes.

Octopus is a color-changing mollusk with eight suction-cup-bearing tentacles; it's the most intelligent invertebrate.

Jellyfish is one of the world's most ancient animals.
It has a soft, jelly-like "bell" and tentacles.

Squid have three hearts. They can swim faster than any other invertebrate. Deep water squid have glow-in-the-dark organs.

Squid have three hearts. They can swim faster
than any other invertebrate. Deep water squid
have glow-in-the-dark organs.

Dolphins are intelligent, vocal, and social.
They have 2 stomachs, and they never chew
their food.

There are over 500 species of shark. Sharks do not have bones. They can be weird and wonderful!

Hammerhead sharks are known for their unique head shape and wide-set eyes. Their eye placement gives them a full 360-degree view.

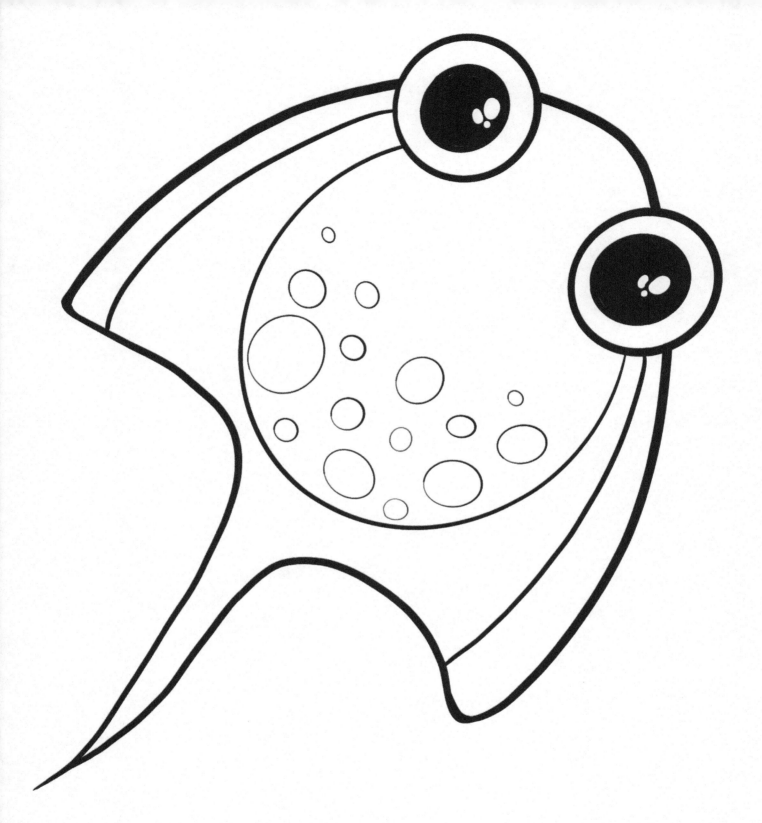

Stingrays have wide, flat bodies and long, sharp, venomous spines on their tails. They are closely related to sharks.

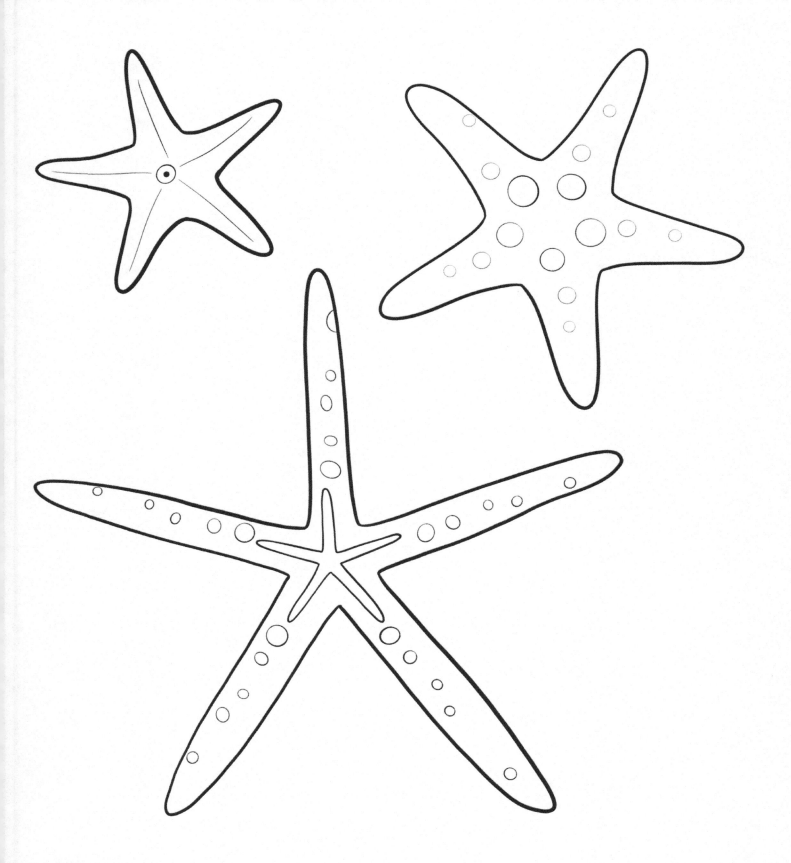

Starfish or sea stars can regenerate their own arms.
They have no brain or blood but have 5 eyes.

Crabs are decapods, meaning they have 10 legs.
Crabs can walk in all directions but mostly walk
and run sideways. Female crabs can release
1000 to 2000 eggs at once.

The Hermit crab belongs to the same family as lobsters, shrimp, and crabs. Hermit crabs carry their homes around on their backs until they outgrow them and move into new ones.

A shrimp is a small shellfish with long legs, and a
long body that has a hard casing.
Shrimp don't have a skeleton!

Sea urchins are covered with long and movable spines. These spines help them move and keep enemies away.

Blue Whale is the world's largest marine animal.
It Can Weigh as Much as 30 Elephants.

Orca is a toothed, predatory black-and-white whale. Orcas live in small groups called pods. They are highly intelligent and have the second largest brain of any animal.

Sea turtles have been on earth for so long. They have lived during the time of the dinosaurs! Sea turtles can hold their breath for five hours underwater.

Coral is a small animal that attaches itself to rocks, building a hard skeleton. More than 25% of all ocean animals need Coral reefs to survive.

Clams cannot smell, taste, feel, hear or see. A clam has a shiny and smooth shell, whereas an oyster shell is more calcified and rough.

Oysters are known for producing pearls, while clams do not. Oysters have three hearts and colorless blood!

Oysters are known for producing pearls, while clams
do not. Oysters have three hearts and colorless blood!

Nautilus move by blowing out water.
They have 90 tentacles and a beak.

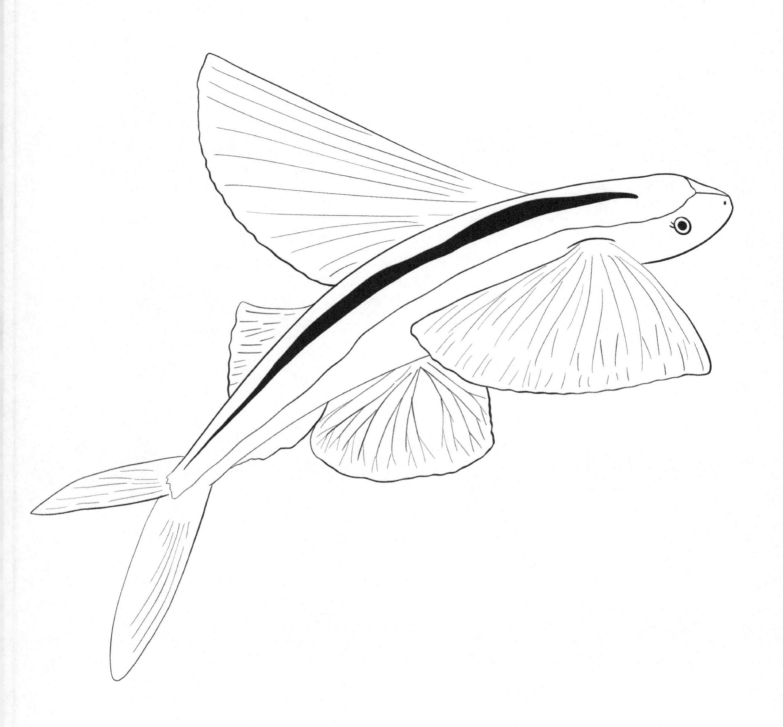

Flying fish do not actually fly by flapping wings as birds do. In fact, they jump from the water and use their fins to glide through the air.

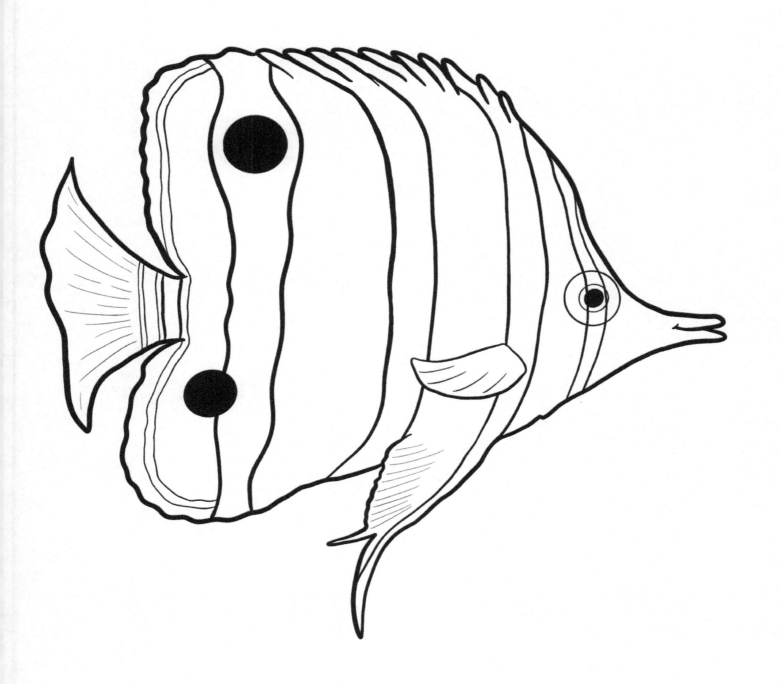

Butterflyfish are bright and colorful, with patterns on their bodies similar to butterflies.

Butterflyfish are bright and colorful, with patterns on their bodies, similar to butterflies.

The Moorish Idol is a fish found on many coral reefs.
It has bars of black, white, and yellow on its body.

Lionfish is a venomous fish with a brownish-red and white-striped body and sharp poisonous spiny fins. Lionfish are nocturnal.

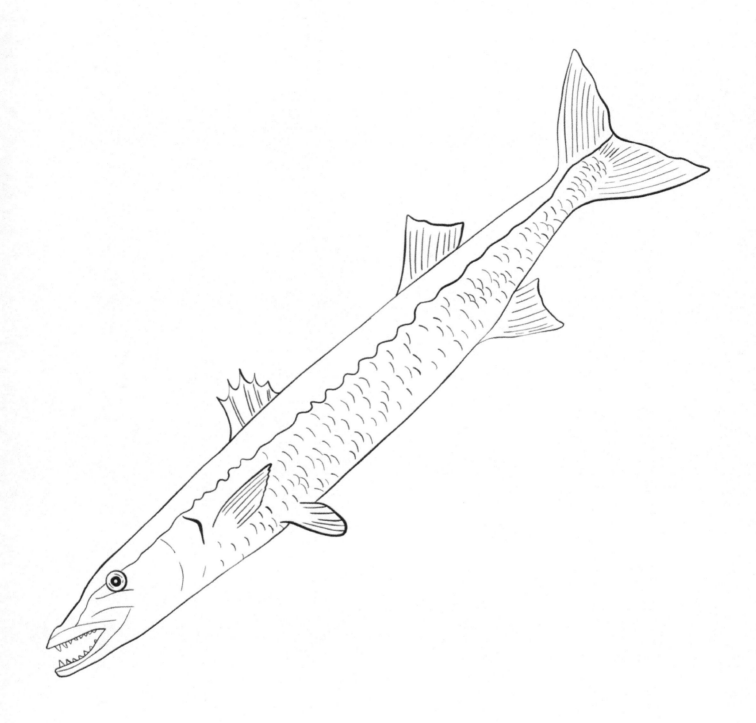

A barracuda, or Cuda for short, is also called the "Tiger of the Sea". The barracuda has a long, thin body that makes it an excellent fast swimmer.

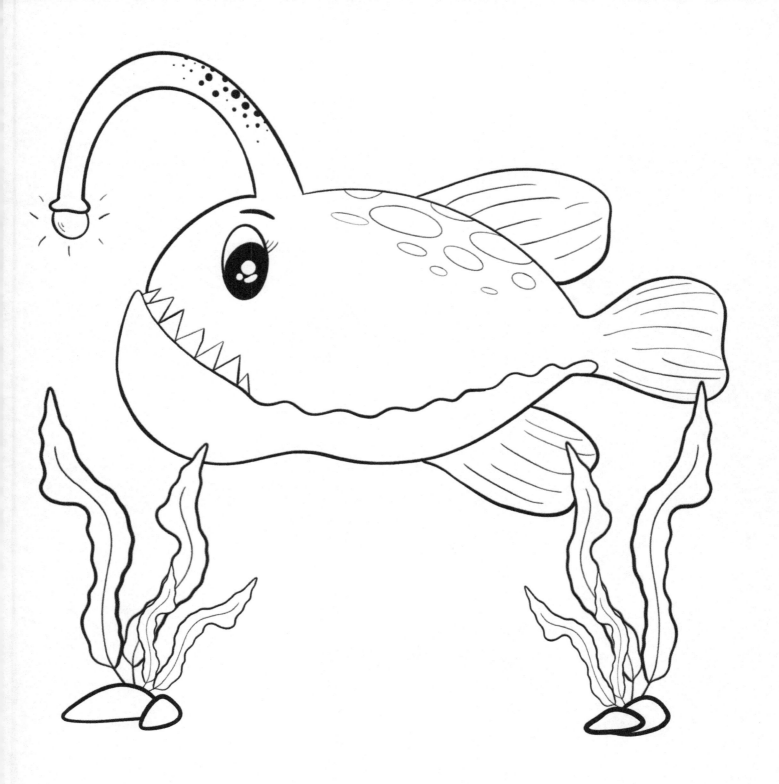

Anglerfish live in the deep sea. They have a rod-like appendage on their head to lure in prey. Some anglerfish can produce their own source of light.

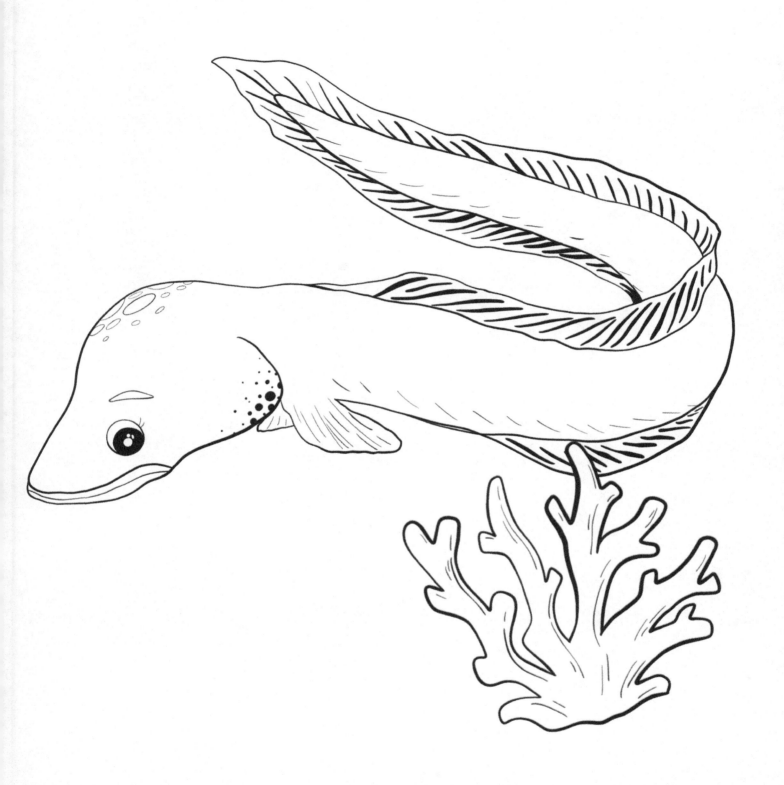

Eel is a long-bodied fish. They can swim
backward and forward and live up to 70 years!

Seals are mammals that live mostly in cold seas.
Their skin is usually brown, gray, or black.
Mothers and pups bond with a unique call.

Walrus is a large Arctic marine mammal with long tusks and whiskers. They can stay underwater for up to half an hour!

The Beluga is an Arctic whale. Beluga whales are slow swimmers. They are very social and the most vocal of all whales.

Narwhals live in the Arctic waters.
They change color as they grow older.
Only male narwhals have a tusk.

Penguins are birds, but they cannot fly.
They are, however, expert swimmers. To save energy,
they slide on their bellies across the snow.

Activity time!

CONNECT THE DOTS

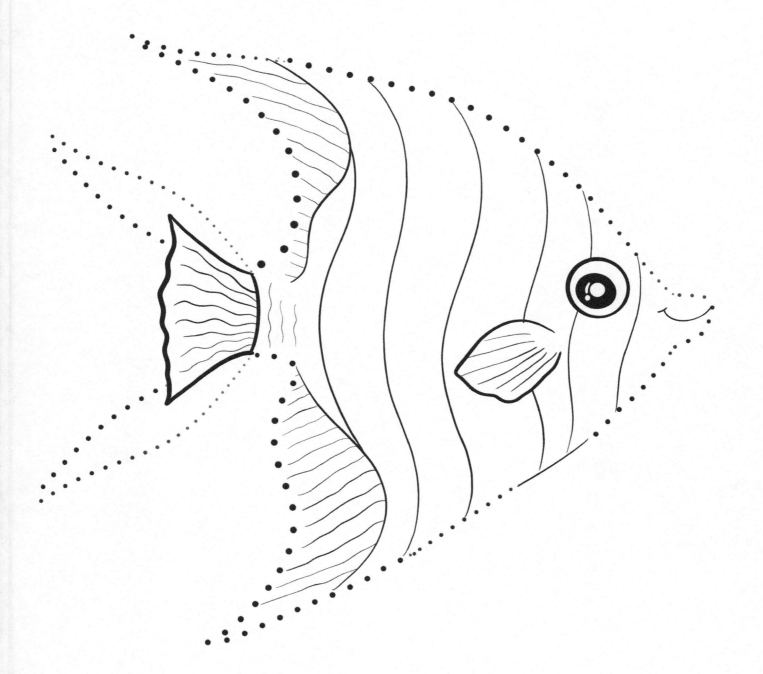

Hello! Color and give it a name!

Hi! Color and give it a name!

‒ ‒

Hi! Color and give it a home!

YOU ARE A-MAZE-ING

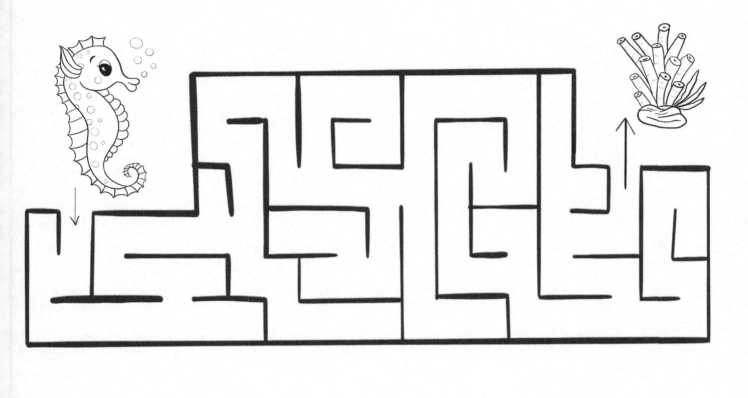

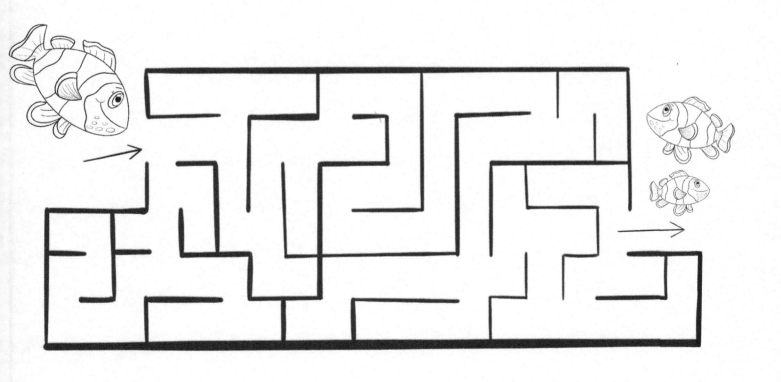

Count and Color

SPOT 7 DIFFERENCES

GUESS THE ANIMAL

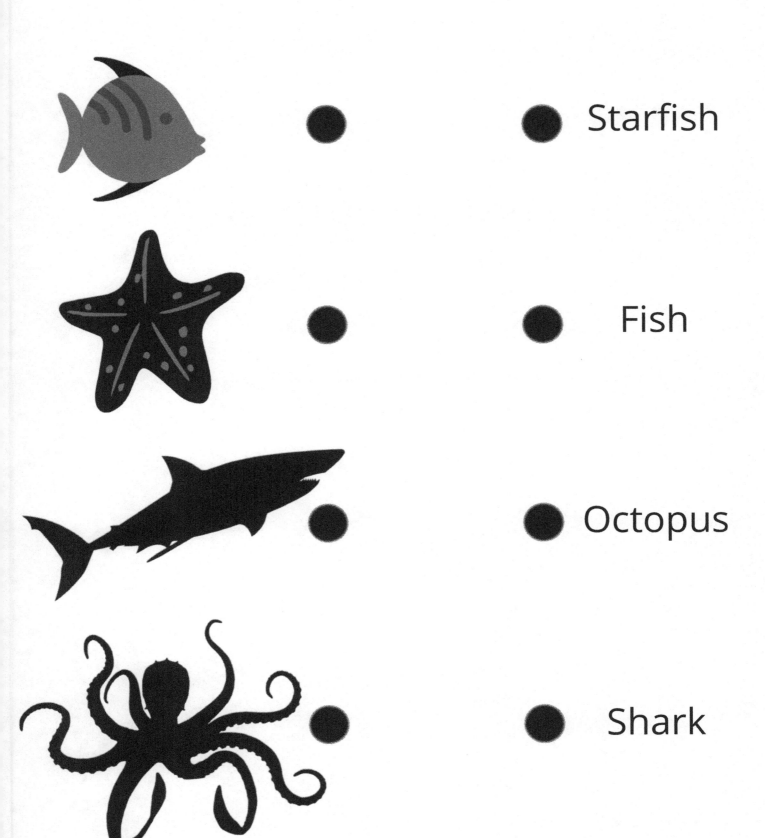

Starfish

Fish

Octopus

Shark

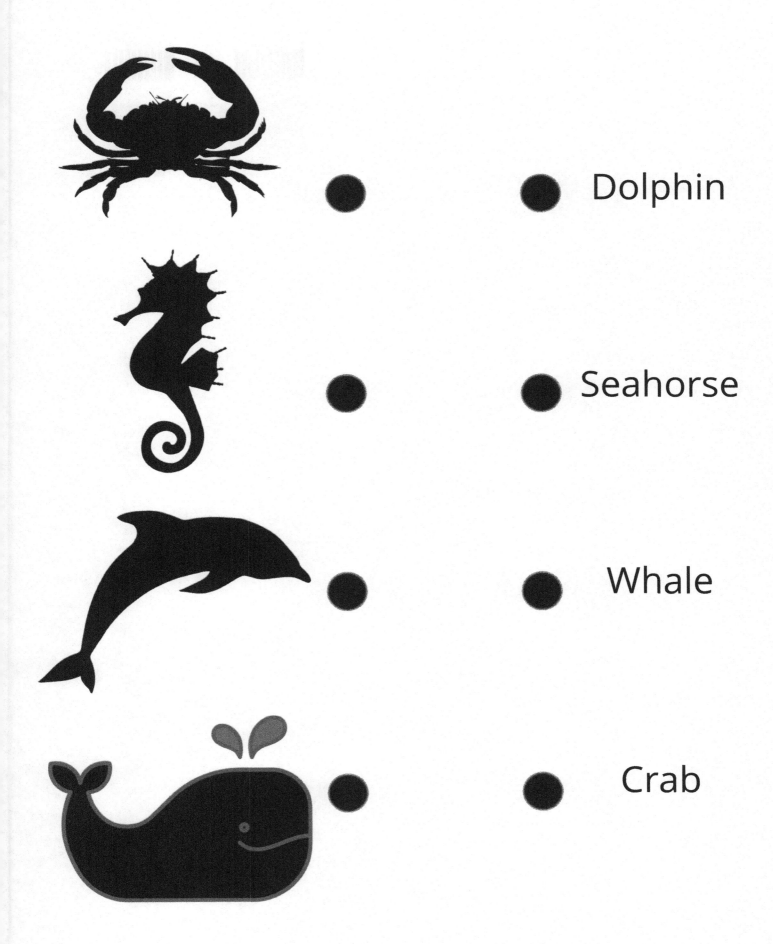

Dolphin

Seahorse

Whale

Crab

Word Search

```
B  H  Y  Q  G  N  Z  T  G  O  L  D  F  I  S  H  X  C  E  H
D  J  V  J  A  V  J  T  R  H  S  H  R  I  M  P  G  L  V  N
L  M  O  U  L  U  E  V  G  A  G  A  H  C  M  Q  S  A  C  V
A  Q  Y  S  E  A     T  U  R  T  L  E  M  R  P  H  M  I  U
A  Q  S  U  B  X  Y  G  S  T  A  R  F  I  S  H  A  Z  P  C
P  N  T  C  T  W  K  J  E  L  L  Y  F  I  S  H  R  U  S  Y
Q  O  E  K  A  M  R  N  S  K  S  C  T  K  C  P  K  O  N  T
S  T  R  R  W  B  B  M  A  D  E  K  P  E  P  V  T  J  K  J
N  A  S  G  V  E  Q  Y  R  O  A  A  Q  R  T  L  D  L  V  E
O  C  T  O  P  U  S  V  D  L  L  K  H  S  R  Z  N  N  C  H
M  G  L  W  B  G  Q  S  I  P  L  O  T  U  N  A  Z  S  K  R
M  C  P  O  R  C  A  W  N  H  Y  N  S  W  X  C  P  V  F  J
A  F  I  S  H  T  U  E  E  I  Y  Y  H  H  T  N  H  J  P  H
T  C  R  A  B  D  W  M  B  N  Y  Z  E  A  O  O  H  J  C  Q
G  O  L  H  L  R  E  M  K  P  M  Z  L  L  O  N  Z  N  K  U
M  N  H  K  P  N  R  Y  N  Z  L  U  L  E  K  Z  H  S  O  Q
A  R  V  A  Z  F  J  Z  S  Q  U  I  D  O  J  S  O  V  X  M
B  X  S  O  B  S  E  A  H  O  R  S  E  H  B  S  V  R  I  V
W  F  U  G  F  T  F  E  P  R  J  N  K  Z  F  E  F  U  N  L
I  U  S  J  U  T  C  R  I  X  I  N  X  L  V  O  L  G  X  X
```

SHRIMP, SQUID, SEAHORSE, CLAM, SHARK, TUNA, SEA TURTLE, SHELL, JELLYFISH, STARFISH, DOLPHIN, WHALE, SARDINE, GOLDFISH, OCTOPUS, OYSTER, FISH, SEAL, CRAB, ORCA

Solution

B	H	Y	Q	G	N	Z	T	**G**	**O**	**L**	**D**	**F**	**I**	**S**	**H**	X	**C**	E	H
D	J	V	J	A	V	J	T	R	H	**S**	**H**	**R**	**I**	**M**	**P**	G	**L**	V	N
L	M	**O**	U	L	U	E	V	G	A	G	A	H	C	M	Q	**S**	**A**	C	V
A	Q	**Y**	**S**	**E**	**A**		**T**	**U**	**R**	**T**	**L**	**E**	M	R	P	**H**	**M**	I	U
A	Q	**S**	U	B	X	Y	G	**S**	**T**	**A**	**R**	**F**	**I**	**S**	**H**	**A**	Z	P	C
P	N	**T**	C	T	W	K	**J**	**E**	**L**	**L**	**Y**	**F**	**I**	**S**	**H**	**R**	U	S	Y
Q	O	**E**	K	A	M	R	N	**S**	K	**S**	C	T	K	C	P	**K**	O	N	T
S	T	**R**	R	W	B	B	M	**A**	D	**E**	K	E	P	E	P	T	J	K	J
N	A	S	G	V	E	Q	Y	**R**	**O**	**A**	A	Q	R	T	L	D	L	V	E
O	**C**	**T**	**O**	**P**	**U**	**S**	V	**D**	**L**	**L**	K	H	S	R	Z	N	N	C	H
M	G	L	W	B	G	Q	S	**I**	**P**	L	O	**T**	**U**	**N**	**A**	Z	S	K	R
M	C	P	**O**	**R**	**C**	**A**	W	**N**	**H**	Y	N	**S**	**W**	X	C	P	V	F	J
A	**F**	**I**	**S**	**H**	T	U	E	**E**	**I**	Y	Y	**H**	**H**	T	N	H	J	P	H
T	**C**	**R**	**A**	**B**	D	W	M	**B**	**N**	Y	Z	**E**	**A**	O	O	H	J	C	Q
G	O	L	H	L	R	E	M	K	P	M	Z	**L**	**L**	O	N	Z	N	K	U
M	N	H	K	P	N	R	Y	N	Z	L	U	**L**	**E**	K	Z	H	S	O	Q
A	R	V	A	Z	F	J	Z	**S**	**Q**	**U**	**I**	**D**	O	J	S	O	V	X	M
B	X	S	O	B	**S**	**E**	**A**	**H**	**O**	**R**	**S**	**E**	H	B	S	V	R	I	V
W	F	U	G	F	T	F	E	P	R	J	N	K	Z	F	E	F	U	N	L
I	U	S	J	U	T	C	R	I	X	I	N	X	L	V	O	L	G	X	X

SHRIMP, SQUID, SEAHORSE, CLAM, SHARK, TUNA, SEA TURTLE, SHELL, JELLYFISH, STARFISH, DOLPHIN, WHALE, SARDINE, GOLDFISH, OCTOPUS, OYSTER, FISH, SEAL, CRAB, ORCA

OCEAN ANIMALS

CERTIFICATE OF COMPLETION

PRESENTED TO

FOR OUTSTANDING PERFORMANCE

SIGNATURE

Nouha Gallery

DATE

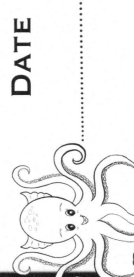

Thank you so much for choosing my Ocean Animals Coloring Book!

As an independent author, every review is incredibly important to me. Please consider taking one minute from your time to share your experience on Amazon and help other parents feel confident about choosing this coloring book. I read every review and appreciate your feedback. Thank you again for your purchase and for supporting independent authors like me.

If you'd like to leave a review, please go to https://amzn.to/3H8fVII , or scan the QR code below.

Like this book? Scan me to find
more titles by Nouha Gallery!

Made in the USA
Las Vegas, NV
29 November 2023

81663818R00057